MANIFESTOS FOR THE 21ST CENTURY

SERIES EDITORS: URSULA OWEN AND JUDITH VIDAL-HALL

Free expression is as high on the agenda as it has ever been, though not always for the happiest of reasons. Here, distinguished writers address the issue of censorship in a complex and fragile world where people with widely different cultural habits and beliefs are living in close proximity, where offence is easily taken, and where words, images and behaviour are coming under the closest scrutiny. These books will surprise, clarify and provoke in equal measure.

Index on Censorship is the only international magazine promoting and protecting free expression. A haven for the censored and silenced, it has built an impressive track record since it was founded 35 years ago, publishing some of the finest writers, sharpest analysts and foremost thinkers in the world. In this series with Seagull Books, the focus will be on questions of rights, liberties, tolerance, silencing, censorship and dissent.

TAKING

offence

CASPAR MELVILLE

LONDON NEW YORK CALCUTTA

Seagull Books 2009

Text © Caspar Melville 2009
Illustrations © New Humanist/Martin Rowson

ISBN-13 978 1 9064 9 702 6

British Library Cataloguing-in-Publication Data
A catalogue record for this book is available
from the British Library

Typeset and designed by Seagull Books, Calcutta, India
Printed in Calcutta at Rockwel Offset

CONTENTS

Controversial cover from New Humanist *magazine, November 2007, which offended many humanists, with cover art by Martin Rowson.*

IN THE WAKE OF 9/11

The towers of the World Trade Center in
New York cast a longer shadow now than
they ever did when they were standing. Our
political and cultural agenda has been
twisted and contorted by the fallout of 11
September 2001 in ways that Osama Bin
Laden cannot have imagined in his wildest
dreams, and the smouldering embers of
that day of destruction continue to waft
toxic fumes over the West.

What 9/11 has bequeathed the world of
cultural and political journalism in which I

work is a twisted kind of thematic coherence that constrains our ways of thinking and provides a predictable track along which debates are forced to run. The themes thus entwined include religion, violence, the nature and future of civilization: abstract themes shot through with a new urgency as they appear to be linked to our very survival. Philosophical and theoretical debates about these matters have taken on a new urgency, but also a futile ambition, as every argument comes to be judged by whether it defends 'Western civilization' or gives succour to terrorists. Terrorist violence has, in a way, revitalized debate, appearing to resolve the issue that always troubled the intellectual: how can we make our discussions relevant to the real world? After all, what could be more relevant than the need to save ourselves and our culture?

But the post-9/11 debate has not confined itself to thinking only about how to

prevent terrorist violence; it has pulled into
its vortex pre-existing debates of long
standing about the relation between religion and secularism, about identity and difference, and about the limits of free speech
in a multicultural society. Essential debates
to have, yet these discussions too readily
take on a kind of theatrical portentousness;
in the attempt to measure up to 9/11, they
are themselves wrapped in the bellicose
rhetoric and the simplifications and hyper-
bole of war. As we are encouraged to believe
that we have reached a 'tipping point', a
decisive moment in the battle between our
civilization and those who would destroy it,
the kind of apocalyptic end-timer logic that
galvanizes the evangelical right in the US
has taken hold. 'Emotional outrage,' writes
Thomas Hegghammer, author of *Jihad in
Saudi Arabia*: *Violence and Pan-Islamism since
1979* (forthcoming), 'prevents us from see-
ing clearly' (2008) This is a situation that

eminently suits extremists and dogmatists, and makes subtlety, complexity and doubt—the essential tools for negotiating the messy realm of human affairs—look like cowardice or treason. It is the moment in which the propagandist flourishes.

Take as an example Geert Wilders' 'film' *Fitna* (2008). Wilders, a populist right-wing Dutch MP and friend of the filmmaker Theo Van Gogh, who was murdered by a Muslim fanatic for his offences against Islam, released *Fitna* on the Internet in June 2008 as a self-declared act of defiance against a murderous threat to liberty and the West. A clear act of provocation, the film was met with a muted response, although Wilders continues to require 24-hour police protection and has recently been indicted, in absentia, by Jordan for crimes against Islam.

Fitna—not so much a film as a cut-and-paste web montage about the length of a

Bjork video—intercuts verses from the
Quran calling for violence against non-
believers with images culled from news
footage of terrorist attacks: planes hitting
the Towers in New York in 2001; bodies laid
out after the Madrid bombings of 2005; a
double-decker bus with its top ripped off in
London's Tavistock Square on 7 July 2007.
These are further spliced with the video sui-
cide notes of bombers, the 'live' beheading
of Nick Berg, obscene pronouncements
from assorted imams—as well as Iran's
President Ahmadinejad—on the need to
murder Jews and obliterate Israel and the
inevitable global triumph of Islam, and of
Muslim protesters carrying signs embla-
zoned with slogans such as 'Freedom can go
to hell,' 'Islam will conquer the world' and
'Death to the infidels.' This footage is inter-
spersed with official-looking charts showing
the exponential growth of the Muslim
populations in the Netherlands and across
Europe, the most recent numbers so high

that the graph streaks up and onward and out of sight.

Fitna closes on a call to action: Hitler was defeated, Communism vanquished, now 'Islamization' must be stopped or . . . and here the camera zooms in on a cartoon image of the Prophet Muhammad, whose turban is a bomb superimposed on the Quran. The fuse on the bomb burns down to nothing and the clock on the screen ticks down to zero. Boom!

Fitna is a crude and revolting piece of propaganda, stoking anti-Muslim senti-ment, homogenizing and caricaturing a re-ligion of billions, and stopping not far short of recommending violent retaliation. And yet there's no better example of the way the drama and shared trauma of 9/11 and the other terror attacks have licensed a certain kind of hyperbolic argumentation. Or a clearer articulation of the way different arguments have, under the pressure of overheated calls to defend civilization, become shackled together. Because, of course, this is not the first time we have seen the cartoon of Muhammad with his turban-bomb. It is one of the 12 cartoons published by the Danish newspaper *Jyllands-Posten* in 2005 that triggered a wave of complaint, protest and violence across the world and resulted in dozens of deaths—perhaps as many as 136 according to the website *Cartoon Body Count*—most of them Muslims who died at the hands of the police forces of Islamic states.

Using the unifying theme of Islam, Wilders' deployment of this image knits together the issue of terrorist violence with that of free speech and offence. Just as it is impossible to step out from under the weight of 9/11 when discussing global terrorism, the Danish cartoons have come to dominate and stand for the contemporary debate around free speech and offence.

The consequence of this is that there is an assumption that taking offence is something inherent in Islam, that Muslim intolerance can only lead to violence and an attack on our very way of life, and that taking a stand in favour of absolute free speech and the right to offend is somehow to take a stand against terrorism. Such an impression is reinforced by the fact that Wilders gained a great deal of publicity for his film, including flattering portraits in the *Spectator* and the *Wall Street Journal*, and an appearance on BBC Radio 4's *The Choice*, where he discussed why he made the 'brave decision' to put his own life at risk. In case you are wondering, it was, he said, to save Western 'Judaeo-Christian' civilization.

To make any kind of sense of these vital issues, these arguments need to be untwined. As the editor of a sceptical rationalist magazine, it is my professional duty to criticize and, at times, to mock religion and pious attitudes in general. If it is the case that certain kinds of attitudes inspired by religion are dangerous or ludicrous, it is my right and my duty to say so. But the duty to think freely, to be sceptical of all dogma, also applies to this 'common sense' interpretation of Islam as a de facto threat to free speech, or the prime mover in the emergence of our contemporary thin-skinned culture.

It is easy and tempting to fall for the propaganda that pins violent intolerance on Islam and calls for a defence of 'our' civilization against 'theirs'. This licenses a kind of cultural jingoism as we launch into a defence of 'our way of life', label our enemy with all the attributes we like least about ourselves and misrepresent the threat to free speech.

Religiously inspired violence is a genuine, terrifying threat, but, though jihadi threats and violence have taken the head-

9

lines in recent years, it is hardly a problem confined to Islam, or even, ultimately, to religious communities. Throughout the world, aggrieved groups are able to rally and incite mobs to respond with loud protests and physical threats to any perceived insult, however slight or mistaken. Sometimes merely to follow a different religion, or none at all, is enough. The most recent outbreak of the long-simmering violence against the Christian population in the Indian state of Orissa—many of whom are converts from Hinduism, from lower castes—that has led to 36 murders and the displacement of tens of thousands has been undertaken by Hindus rallying around the cry to 'Defend Mother India' apparently on a mission to purify what they perceive to be a Hindu country. Closer to home, the response of Birmingham's Sikh community to the staging of the controversial play *Behzti* in 2004—a large violent mob descended upon the theatre, disrupted the performance and engaged in running battles with riot police—suggests the intensity of feeling and the willingness to vent that feeling that can be unleashed by contemporary perceptions of offensiveness. Within this process, self-appointed spokesmen and spurious 'human rights' groups have emerged to publicize incidents of offence and stoke up anger around them, often making adept use of digital technology such as e-mail lists and blogs. As claims of offence seem to reap rewards—governments and local authorities keen to appear culturally sensitive and cultural institutions and businesses keen to avoid controversy or violence respond to declarations of offence with apologies and withdrawals—these groups are emboldened and claims of offence become more frequent, more aggressive.

In 2006, an exhibition at India House in London by India's most eminent painter

M. F. Husain was shut down because of vociferous complaints from an organization calling itself Hindu Human Rights and threats of violence from outraged individuals. This incident featured the now typical mix of these sorts of incidents: the language of human rights and anti-racism broadcast by pressure groups claiming legitimacy to speak for 'minority communities', allied with threats of intimidation or violence from individuals which, while officially disavowed by these groups, is also used by them as evidence of the depth of hurt feeling.

A prime exploiter of this tactic in the UK is the evangelical pressure group Christian Voice. Although widely thought of as an embarrassment and a crank by mainstream Christians, armed only with the Bible, a computer and an absolute belief in his mission to cure Britain of sin, its leader Stephen Green has achieved a high public profile by claiming to speak on behalf of British Christians, voicing their outrage at perceived offences against the faith. Green cut his teeth on the protest against *Jerry Springer the Opera*, and found himself invited onto local and national media as a putative representative of Christian outrage, While that protest gave rise to little more violence than some lobby-jostling, Green's more recent pronouncements and campaigns carry a more sinister undertone. In November 2008, a book signing in Cardiff by Welsh poet Patrick Jones was hurriedly cancelled by the booksellers Waterstone's following the receipt of complaints from Christians who claimed Jones' poetry was blasphemous. These complaints, some threatening disruption and violence, were coordinated by Green through his e-mail distribution list; Waterstone's took the threats seriously enough to cancel the event. In a press statement, Waterstone's argued that though they supported free speech—the book remained on sale—they felt they could not risk the possibility of disruption at the store. Through the simple expedient of sending an outraged e-mail, laced with a threat of violence, campaigns like this can achieve a great deal with very little expense or effort. Jones' recent visit to the UK in February 2009 aroused widespread public controversy.

Such specifically faith-based protests are merely a part of what the art critic Robert Hughes dubbed the 'culture of complaint' that seems to define our current period. We have been encouraged, indeed encouraged ourselves, to believe that we have the right to complain whenever we encounter something we don't like as long as we can couch it in terms of offence. Not liking something is a matter of opinion, whereas offending someone is now taken as an attack on their very identity, proof that injury has been caused and recompense is required. This is fuelled by a media that revels in such trumped-up claims and by the easy-access technology of e-mail and blogging that allows instant and unaccountable expression of self-righteous outrage. Such a combination is what underlies the furore around the 'Andrew Sachs Affair' in the UK towards the end of 2008. It led to high-profile broadcasters Jonathan Ross and Russell Brand being censured for a tasteless joke on their radio show. Though the show received a mere handful of complaints after airing, once the story was picked up by the press and broadcast through the blogosphere the BBC received more than 30,000 complaints, the vast majority by e-mail, all protesting the apparent offensiveness of the gag, though it was targeted very specifically at one person, not a group or religion.

Looked at from this perspective, Islamic outrage of the kind that greeted the

Danish cartoons, though it differs in terms of scale and especially the level of violence it is prepared to deploy, is one part of a much wider trend. And though we are appalled, as we should be, by the actual and threatened violence against those perceived as having insulted Islam—including the foiled plot to assassinate one of the Danish cartoonists in February 2008, or the fire-bombing of the publisher of *The Jewel of Medina* in London in September 2008, or the repeated threats made on the life of the odious Wilders—we nevertheless need to acknowledge the part that we have played in creating this culture of complaint and over-sensitivity. We need to resist the lure of hasty self-congratulation and the boiling down of complex political and historical processes into slogan-friendly absolutes; to resist, too, the lure of the propagandists that lets us off having to face our own role in nurturing the threats to life and liberty that stalk us now. It is convenient, but in my view fatal, to pin the blame on Islam.

An example of what I have in mind is provided by the US historian Joan Scott in her analysis of the French headscarf ban of 2004. The ban, which outlawed the wearing of religious symbols such as the headscarf in state schools, was mooted by its supporters as justified on the basis of the principle of *laicité* or secularism, which is 'invoked by its proponents as an absolute value [although] very little regard is paid either to the historical evolution of the idea or the current context in which it is deployed' (2008). Scott directs her attention to precisely this, and finds that, in contradiction of its own rhetoric, French secularism is partial and, as a consequence of the way it arose against the dominance of the Catholic Church, continues to accommodate Christianity in particular ways. It is 'inconsistent and variable' and therefore the attempt to apply non-negotiable rules solely to Muslims is unfair and 'can only be perceived as discriminatory'.

For Scott, this misrepresentation of secularism as absolute and ahistorical has an obvious ideological purpose: to project the myth of France as 'one and indivisible', thus allowing the nation to avert its gaze from and avoid the implications of the fact that 'the problems of diversity and difference', in particular, economic and social discrimination and the poverty and marginalization of former colonial subjects, 'have been avoided rather addressed'.

Such a sleight of hand, that projects an implicitly pristine 'Western Culture' under threat from outsiders who don't understand our ways, is what characterizes much of the current debate around offence. The notion of fundamental incompatibility between the 'free' West and Islam serves to conceal the continuation of inequality and prejudice, and also conceals the depredations of free speech and the emergence of pious notions of identity and respect we have allowed and encouraged in our own institutions and civic fabric. If we want to undo them, the first task is to acknowledge our own complicity.

THE FREE SOCIETY: MY PART IN ITS DOWNFALL
To understand where our contemporary concern with offence comes from, and what responsibility we might have to shoulder for the state we find ourselves in, it is probably right that I start with myself. Rather than exemplary, I believe my case is fairly typical (at least of others of my class and politics) and I cannot exclude myself from the blame I believe our Western culture bears for stimulating, encouraging, even nurturing, the idea that offence is a harm from which we should be protected.

I have spent the past seven years working as a journalist and editor, and jihadi violence has given my career a kind of punctuated equilibrium. I joined the online political magazine *openDemocracy* a couple of weeks before 9/11; my first substantial task was to edit and publish incredulous eyewitness accounts of the Towers' destruction, many on the plaintive keynote theme of that moment: 'Why do they hate us?' After the 2004 bombings at Madrid's Atocha station, the first major jihadi terrorist atrocity in Europe, I spent several months organizing and publishing the 'After Madrid' debate and commissioning articles on 'Terrorism and Democracy'. The week after I joined *New Humanist* magazine as editor in July 2005, I heard the curiously innocuous thud of the Number 30 bus exploding in Tavistock Square three streets away from my office. Religiously inspired violence forced itself into my life, as it had with everyone else, and cast a queasy new light on everything I had valued and believed up to that point.

In 2001, I had watched the second plane—the one which, as Martin Amis has written, in the deliberateness of its banking, announced the intentions and competence of the jihadis (2008)—hit the South Tower of the World Trade Center on the computer screen in the library of Goldsmiths College in Lewisham. I was there finishing the final chapter of my Ph.D. dissertation, putatively a social history of nightclub culture in London, but also a kind of love letter to London's multiculturalism. In its depiction of the benefits of cultural mixture, the thrill of hybridity and the poverty of racist monoculturalism, I argued that not only was cultural mixture a fact in the streets of London, it was also a huge benefit and promise for the future. Events since then have forced me to reevaluate my rosy assessment of multiculturalism.

The shadow of terrorist attacks on Western soil, which so many have argued is a consequence of over-liberal immigration policies and an institutionalization of cultural relativism, has fallen on my own intellectual history and commitments in ways that suggest the uncomfortable possibility that the commitment to identity politics, political correctness and multiculturalism might have been at least part of the problem.

In 1989, a year after the publication of his novel *The Satanic Verses*, Salman Rushdie was placed under a fatwa issued by Ayatollah Khomeini that put a price on his head and urged all pious Muslims to kill him. This event arguably announced the arrival of a new era in global politics. Certainly, it is the point at which offending Islam became a global capital offence. It also introduced a new word to the political lexicon, at least for non-Muslims, and gave that word—jihad—an ominous new spin. For many, this is the founding moment in the rise of global political Islam, the taster for 9/11 and the test case of the West's commitment to freedom of speech, a test that the West, in scrambling to placate enraged Muslims, flunked. It is certainly true that Rushdie did not receive the public or state support he had every right to expect: denunciations of the act of condemning a foreign national to death for having written something in a novel that some people felt was offensive, were few and far between. The Rushdie fatwa certainly announced a new era of a sort, an era in which Western governments were only too happy to play down the value of free expression in favour of *realpolitik* in the interests of social cohesion at home and international trade and cooperation.

But whether this was the first sign of a specifically religious agenda is not so clear.

The writer and commentator Kenan Malik
argues that Khomeini's fatwa had less to do
with religion than with the fact that he was
keen to shore up his flagging domestic support a decade after the revolution in Iran
(2009, forthcoming). Khomeini also wanted
to undermine Saudi Arabia's dominance of
international Islamism. While the Saudis
had well-funded networks, they could not
compete with the global attention garnered
by the Rushdie headlines. Once it was clear
from the Western response that claims of injury would get a hearing, even concessions,
the die was cast. The fatwa, in Malik's view,
was a political act to do with domestic and
global power that merely drew on Islam for
its justification. It had little to do with Allah
and everything to do with expediency, and
the offence Rushdie apparently caused to
the sensibilities of all Muslims was a carefully
staged sham.

The real consequence of the fatwa, be-
yond the devastating impact on the lives of

Rushdie and others who had been involved
with the book's production—the Japanese
translator Hitoshi Igarashi was murdered;
the book's Norwegian publisher William
Nygaard shot and seriously wounded; the
Italian translator stabbed—was to stand as
an example of how useful putatively
wounded religious sentiment would prove
in political ambitions, and particularly how
such matters sent Western states into confu-
sion and panic. What was striking about
that time was the relative absence of arguments about the absolute right of free expression. This is partly because, despite the
religious rhetoric of the Ayatollah, the fatwa
brought into opposition two contemporary,
secular Western values: the right to free expression and the newly emerging, distinctly
modern and hitherto barely articulated
right to claim special exception and special
treatment based on particular forms of
identity. This new sense of 'rights', though
increasingly adopted and exploited by

religion and global Islamism, originated in the West around very different forms of collective identity, in particular race and ethnicity.

In fact, the fatwa, consciously or not, drew on all the intellectual resources of what had been emerging, particularly in the US, for some time—what we might call the 'offence industry'. It originates in the emergence of a new form of fundamentalism that is not about religion per se, but about identity. It invokes the notion that you have the right to be protected from the harm visited on you by being offended. This is not something that is inherent to any religion, but is a consequence of a new kind of fundamentalism and a new form of literalism.

INSTITUTIONALIZING THIN SKIN

When I was an undergraduate studying American Literature I spent 1989–90, the year of the fatwa, at the University of California Santa Cruz. This was perhaps the highpoint of identity politics on US campuses and UCSC was widely regarded as the centre of leftist radicalism and identitarian politics. One of the classes I attended, taught by the black activist and radical lesbian writer Gloria T. Hull, was the graduate class 'Black Women Writers'. I was one of only two men—both white—who signed up for the course, a number that halved after the first week when the other man got cold feet. The basis of the course was readings from the corpus of radical black feminism—bell hooks, Barbara Christian, Gloria Anzaldua, Angela Davis—and it encouraged a feminist-centred approach to African-American literature and history.

The course was fascinating but increasingly contentious. It became dominated by a vituperative debate about the politics of identity, pivoting around skin tones. Central to the African-American literary tradition is an exploration of the intricacies of racist taxonomies: the way Africans and their descendants were rated by the degree to which their skin differed from white skin, the bizarre mathematics of Octoroon and Quadroon and mulatto, the distinction between those Africans granted limited access to whites through domestic servitude—frequently the lighter skinned—and those destined for a life in the fields. Central to narratives about race in the nineteenth and early-twentieth century, such as Nella Larsen's novel *Passing* (1929) and the John M. Stahl film *Imitation of Life* (1934), was the whole dangerous, fascinating and inevitably doomed prospect that some very light-skinned Afro-Americans might, for a time, 'pass' as white. Deconstruction of the figure of the 'tragic mulatto' was central to the course. The critical aspect of this for our purpose was the terms in which the debate played out in the classroom. This was no dry theoretical discussion but a lively, personalized debate about identity, in which accusations of 'essentializing', claims of harm caused by language and an obsession with victimhood, supercharged the atmosphere of the seminar.

Strangely, very little rancour was directed at me—not only a straight white man but a European to boot—but then, not having a personal stake in the issue by virtue of the fact that I was not oppressed, left me on the sidelines. Instead, what played out was a kind of microcosm of the 'narcissism of minor difference' that fractured the European Left in the 1960s and 1970s, with the added potency of race, feminism and queer theory. Underlying the fierce debates was a kind of oppression Top Trumps where each student's personal experiences of oppression were ranked according to a hierarchy within which the 'triple jeopardy' of being black, female and homosexual conferred a certain degree of status. There were very serious issues at stake in these debates, and the work of many of the writers we studied, including Gloria T. Hull, Patricia Bell Scott and Barbara Smith's own edited collection *All the Blacks are Men. All the Women are White. But Some of Us are Brave* (1982), were powerful articulations of the consequence of such multiple oppressions and the attempt to escape them. The course and the politics around it were driven by the noblest motivations, a desire to end inequality and give the downtrodden dignity and a voice.

Yet underlying the debates were two very toxic assumptions. The first: that your right to speak or hold an opinion or to join a particular debate depended on the degree to which you yourself had experienced whatever it was under discussion—which was rarely anything other than oppression. Suffering became not just the reason to listen to someone—a very good reason—but the reason not to disagree with someone.

The second: the implication that discussing these issues, which drew in history, politics and philosophy, was or should be somehow therapeutic. In order to heal the psychic trauma of living under multiple oppression, it was suggested, one had to reclaim one's own right to speak, to remake one's history—and therefore history itself—and to prevent anyone from visiting 'epistemic violence' on you ever again. In this way, although the seminar group was composed of serious, intelligent and diligent graduate students, there was an unmistakable echo of the growing trend in popular culture towards a confessional, self-revelatory tone that was concerned more with healing and compensating victimhood than with the pursuit of knowledge or the dispassionate evaluation of argument. This reinforced what the postcolonial theorist Achille Mbembe has described as the chief constituent of the 'victimary consciousness', 'addiction to the memory of one's own suffering' (in Mongin et al 2006). Education became Oprah-ized.

My seminar was no isolated occurrence. These trends were sweeping the US academy, as a generation of academics and students, disillusioned with formal, usually left-wing politics as a way to change the world, turned to a theoretical mode shot through with the idea that the victims of racism, colonialism and multiple oppression could get restitution and psychic healing through alternative epistemologies and by patrolling the borders of acceptable speech.

The urge to reclaim your own damaged history, a perfectly valid and admirable aim though perhaps better pursued in creative writing or filmmaking, led to an individualization of knowledge and of history, just as the postmodern suspicion of 'meta-narratives' put quotation marks around 'truth'. You could, students were told, find your own truth or make it. And part of this was to be on eternal guard for any threat to your new, self-made identity—the kind of threat that might, for example, come through offensive words, images or ideas. Even a look, coded as an oppressive 'gaze', could be punishable.

Though the reading list of the 'Black Women Writers' course featured many who were associated with traditional Left politics, even communism or socialism, such as the poet Sonia Sanchez and Angela Davis, herself by then a professor at the University of California, it was clear that any sense of collective socialist politics, or even a collective black politics, had lost its traction. If the personal was political, then wasn't the political really personal? The way of doing politics became defined by how adept you were at negotiating the terrain of correct speech, behaviour and opinion.

The consequences of a misplaced comment, a speculative disagreement or,

God forbid, a joke, could be very serious:
personal attack, group disapproval and a
slow grind through the newly empowered
institutional apparatus set up to adjudicate
claims of 'abuse', within which showing
insufficient respect, attacking the identity
that is taken by this new orthodoxy as the
chief constituent of the self, is one of the
most serious offences.

Santa Cruz had by then developed the
kind of register of forbidden words and
sanctions against offensive language,
backed by the threat of disciplinary action,
that the journalist Jonathan Rauch describes in his book *Kindly Inquisitors* (1993).
He cites as an example of the new institutional codes the University of Missouri
Journalism School's 'Dictionary of Caution-
ary Words and Phrases', from which he
quotes:

> *Burly*: An adjective too often associ-
> ated with large black men, implying

ignorance, and considered offensive
in this context.

Buxom: Offensive reference to a
woman's chest. Do not use, See
'Woman'.

Codger: Offensive reference to a sen-
ior citizen.

By the early 1990s, according to Rauch,
professors began to tape their classes in
case they were charged with saying something offensive.

In his book, a staunch defence of what
he calls 'Liberal Science', Rauch speaks up
for the system of argument and verification
that pits arguments against each other in a
way that may cause offence but allows them
to compete on intrinsic merit rather than on
meanings that are distorted and censored
because of special interests. Rauch identifies
three groups whose efforts combined to undermine liberal science and free expression
in particular: the fundamentalists, the

egalitarians and the humanitarians. While
he identifies creationists and other varieties
of religious literalism—including Islamists—
as a significant force in this gagging of public debate, he reserves his strongest
criticisms for the latter two groups, the
'kindly' inquisitors of his title.

These groups, Rauch acknowledges, are
'acting on morally unimpeachable motives;
to protect the weak, to salve hurt feelings,
and to weed out hateful and hurtful ideas'
but, partly because of their morally pure
motives, they represent the most powerful
threat to free speech and reason:

> In the 1980s, it began to be common-
> place for activists and intellectuals
> conspicuously to take offence. Here,
> there and everywhere they were of-
> fended. People began demanding
> public apologies when they were of-
> fended. Often jokes were the target.
> Organised groups—gay activists for

example—began patrolling the
presses and the airwaves for offensive
statements and promptly demanding
apologies or retractions when they
found the cause for complaint.

This, in turn, swelled the ranks of activism
with those predisposed to be offended:

As more and more people realised
that they could win concessions and
moral victories by being offended,
more and more offended people became activists.

These potent claims to offence were
especially prevalent in academia, where the
next generation of lawyers, social workers
and historians were being trained. In the
book *History Lesson: A Race Odyssey* (2008),
classical scholar Mary Lefkowitz tells a story
that encapsulates some of the consequences
of this trend. The book concerns a controversy that arose around the teaching of classical history on the Africana Studies course

at her own university, Wesleyan College.
Lefkowitz discovered that a course called
'Africans in Antiquity' was teaching what
has become known as the 'Stolen Legacy'
perspective, after the book of that title by
George G. M. James (1993). This perspective argues that much of what we celebrate
about the culture of ancient Greece had
been stolen from ancient Egypt, and that
this debt to Africa had gone unacknowl-
edged or was suppressed because of the
innate bias and institutionalized racism of
classical history departments, including
Lefkowitz's.

One core part of this 'Afrocentric' argument was that Aristotle, rather than being
responsible for his own ideas, had lifted
them from Egyptian books he had filched
on visits to the library in Alexandria. The
whole edifice of apparently superior West-
ern-white-civilization was, in fact, built on
the systematic pillaging of African intellec-

tual culture that had then been dismantled by slavery and denied ever since. The symbolic power of such assertions in the frenzied atmosphere of late-twentieth century US racial politics was obvious; the problem was it wasn't true. Lefkowitz knew that Aristotle had died decades before the library at Alexandra was built:

> By letting students believe that [Africans] had a significant cultural influence on Greek civilisation, it seemed to me that we were encouraging our students to believe in a lie.

Lefkowitz later discovered the source of the stolen legacy idea: a long-forgotten historical novel called *Sethos: A History* by Abbé Jean Terrason, written in eighteenth-century France.

Lefkowitz made attempts to raise the issue with her university and wrote several articles about it that brought her some notoriety. She clearly had a stake in the

'classical' version of Classical history, and
the debate she became embroiled in is a
complex one. However, two elements of her
tale stand out. The first: that when she went
public with her complaints, she was sub-
jected to a barrage of personal criticism
that accused her of racism and being part
of a Jewish conspiracy to suppress black
history. Her evidence-based case against the
'stolen legacy' perspective was pushed aside
in favour of a personalized identity-based
battle in which her attack on historical
inaccuracy was perceived as an attack on
the individual identity of others.

Second: when she turned to her university for support—she was in dispute with
another Wesleyan alumni Tony Martin, a
high-profile Afrocentric theorist—the ad-
ministration responded with a blithe relativism, arguing that there were several
possible interpretations of history, each with
their own validity, so they felt they should

not take sides. The dispute moved into the courts. In 1993, Martin issued a lawsuit for libel against her and two others. The case, and a vicious feud with Martin, dragged on for five years until it was finally dismissed. Lefkowitz, who admits she wandered naively into an issue with huge symbolic importance, keeps returning to the simple basis of her disagreement with the Afrocentrists: the evidence does not support their arguments.

In this climate, one of overheated personalized politics and fierce demand for rights, a period defined by what legal philosopher Michael Neumann describes, in his 2006 article 'Respectful Cultures And Disrespectful Cartoons, East Meets West', as a new orthodoxy 'built on an inflated notion of rights and respect, skewed ideas of injury and punishment, and the reliance on "voices" in establishing truths', Lefkowitz's argument, merely a re-statement of the basic values of academic evidence, sounds almost radical: 'The solution is not to argue that all narratives are political and that there is therefore no such thing as truth'. Instead, she argues, academics have to:

> [T]ake responsibility for deciding among various narratives and demonstrate that some are supported by better evidence than others, and that some are even demonstrably false.

But the new orthodoxy allows the perception of offence to trump such trifling considerations.

In her book *Race Experts: How Racial Etiquette, Sensitivity Training, and New Age Therapy Hijacked the Civil Rights Revolution* (2001), historian Elisabeth Lasch-Quinn examines the origins of what she calls 'the diversity industry' which sprang up in the US to service this new orthodoxy of rights and sensitivity. In the mid-1960s, she writes:

> [A]s the civil rights movement lost its direction, universalistic claims for full civic inclusion were replaced by militant assertions of the significance of identity.

Her analysis shows how this idea of identity foregrounded notions of respect, the demand for compensation for perceived suffering and, crucially, drew on and merged with a therapeutic 'new age' culture where the individual becomes the author of their own truth. Within a new industry of diversity training and race sensitivity replete with its army of counsellors, educationalists, diversity trainers and etiquette experts who have taken it upon themselves to re-educate citizens about correct language, correct behaviour and correct attitudes in all matters racial, from the workplace to classrooms, from universities to government departments, difference is 'fatally fetishized'.

This produces a culture where everyone's 'truth' is equally valid, and everyone has the right to be respected, and compensated if they are not. Neumann describes the way in which reason and evidence is degraded in favour of a system of competing self-validating claims:

> That someone says they feel bad is taken to be proof that they feel bad. That someone says their identity has been damaged, or outraged, is proof that this mysterious injury has afflicted them. That someone says an experience has ruined their life proves that their life is ruined and by that experience . . . 'Communities', whose existence is established by the mere assertion that they exist, are known to suffer injuries on the basis of mere assertions coming from someone who merely claims to be a 'member' or 'leader'. This ideology pervades not just public discourse, or

the university campus, but the civil fabric itself. Courts of law have acquired unexpected abilities to determine such subtleties as when an image is degrading.

For both Neumann and Lasch-Quinn the consequences of this withdrawal from the commitment on the one hand to social justice and equality, and on the other to evidence-based argument, have been catastrophic. 'Today,' Lasch-Quinn told one reporter, 'this kind of identity politics stands in for a public philosophy. It's an extraordinary defeat for equality and progress for humanity.' This is the context in which we need to assess what is going on, and how to respond when people take offence and demand respect, because when they do so it is in the language and using the legal precedents pioneered by this new orthodoxy.

A CLASH OF PIETIES

A further element in the story of how good intentions led to bad ideas and worse law comes when this hyper-individualized, thin-skinned culture of victimhood draws on the language of rights. The plea for basic civic rights to be extended to all—a concept developed out of the fight for racial justice in the US and South Africa and the consequences of the Holocaust—has become a call for group and individual rights, for the defence of putatively 'traditional' values and rights, and for compensatory rights. Rather than cleave to a strong minimal version of rights, however, legal systems, particularly in the US, have welcomed rights inflation, notions of psychic harm and the right to restitution as a lucrative opportunity. But the 'rights' on which these claims are based, rights to offend and not to be offended, to be respected and protected from the harm of misrecognition, are illusory. 'Where,' asks Neumann, 'do they come from? Nobody says. These rights compete with each other but without a sound basis on which to adjudicate between them. Inflated rights and inflated notions of respect vie in the public sphere. An absolute relativism reigns: all cultures and persons are imagined to deserve respect, and respecting someone, which is pre-eminently a matter of how you feel about them, is made compulsory and backed by the threat of punishment.

In Neumann's view, what this amounts to is the emergence of a new 'culture of piety' built around the 'bogus value' of respect which becomes a duty. This culture is grounded not in evidence or reason but in:

> Faith—faith in That Which Must
> Be Respected . . . Respect, the fore-
> most value of this culture, translates
> into behaviour as reverence. Disre-
> spect, its foremost sin, becomes
> punishable.

In his prescient essay 'The Politics of Recognition' (1992), philosopher Charles Taylor describes 'a massive subjective turn' in modern culture, and how 'the demand for recognition is now explicit . . . and misrecognition has graduated to the rank of harm.' In Taylor's argument, modern religious identities, no less than New Age communities or sensitivity trainers, compete on the same terrain in the same terms. This means not only that we cannot pin the blame for the emergence of this orthodoxy on religion per se, but that we have to recognize that the problem lies at the core and not the periphery of contemporary culture. The matter cannot be cast as a clash between a stable culture of openness, free speech and the rule of law, and a mediaeval culture of superstition, inequality and intolerance. For Neumann then, the real issue is that the West has put 'ideological weapons in the hands of those it now wants to repel'.

'Having tossed the basic notions of the rule of law in the trashcan,' he concludes, 'they cannot be picked out and held up as shiny western ideals just because it is convenient to do so'.

What emerges out of Neumann's argument is an image not of a clash of fundamentally incompatible civilizations, but a period defined by two kinds of cultures of piety, Islamism and 'political correctness'. Together, these dominate the political landscape and their demands for rights on the one hand and respect on the other are each other's mirror image. As Neumann argues, they share a common heritage in the failed project of universalist secular leftism and have arisen to fill the gap where ideology used to be. What they share is that they are 'incredibly sensitive to what doesn't matter, and incredibly insensitive to what does'. For him, the lesson of the Danish cartoons crisis is 'not that Islam can be offended; it is not a lesson about Islam at all.' Instead, it is a lesson about bad ideologies pitting two versions of individualized identity—the twin pieties of Western identity-speak and Islam—against each other on the global stage.

MULTICULTURALISM: EMPOWERING ISLAM

But how well do these arguments apply outside the US case they address? Arguably, the influence of identity politics and the political correctness industry has been far less outside the US. However, there is an equivalent of these pieties in Europe. The inflation of the political language of 'harm', whether it be caused by smoking, pornography, obesity, bad parenting or binge-drinking, and the rush to legislate against these harms is an analogue of and part of the same trend as the US rights-and-respect industry. And in terms of piety, the equivalent of politically correct piety is, in the British

context, multicultural piety. It shares the
core features of reinforcing a sense of identity at the expense of belonging, of favour-
ing exceptionalism over universality, of
compensating victimhood. It stokes the
inflation of rights, especially the right not
to be offended and to seek compensation
if you are, over any sense of duty or
responsibility.

Multiculturalism, as I mentioned earlier,
is something I grew up with and actively supported. Cultural and racial mixture, in the
context of the racial politics of the 1970s,
from Enoch Powell's 'Rivers of Blood'
speech of 1968 to the race riots of 1980,
1981 and 1985, was something I always felt
needed to be defended and celebrated. It
was the political narrative that ran counter
to the little-Englanders and the anti-immi-
gration bigots and the 'separate but equal'
liberals. That a mixed culture was a good
thing was something we needed to say. As

Salman Rushdie once famously wrote when
he was more sanguine about the benefits of
cultural diversity: 'Melange, hotchpotch, a
bit of this and bit of that is how newness en-
ters the world' (1991). In any case, there is
no culture that has not been mixed, mon-
grel or hybrid. Arguments about cultural
purity or contamination, the multiculturalist argues, are always dangerous political
fantasies. This is where the celebration of
hybridity, syncretism and 'cut-n-mix' culture, the creative practices of the subordi-
nates who remake culture through music,
art and bricolage, as celebrated in the work
of   Stuart Hall, Paul Gilroy and Dick Heb-
dige, makes its important intervention. But
in the case of the UK, there is another kind
of multiculturalism that is as distinct from
the theoretical celebration of difference and
culture mixture as it is from the manifest
fact of diversity: the fact, for example, that
there are 43 different languages spoken at

my local primary school. When we talk about multiculturalism as a piety and a contributor to a loss of faith in reason and evidence and equality, we are addressing multicultural policy.

Multiculturalism has always had its severe critics. In the years following 9/11 and especially 7/7, these voices have reached an hysterical pitch. Most recently, Dominic Grieve, Conservative shadow home secretary in the UK, has spoken of the disaster wrecked on the UK by 'state multiculturalism' and the need to reassert a strong national identity, to include the indigenous white British on the list of distinct cultures that need preservation and respect. But the most powerful criticisms come not from those who never had a stake in anti-racism or a commitment to overcoming narrow versions of British identity, but from those who share the principles that underpin multiculturalism but have come to see its self-defeating nature.

One of these is Kenan Malik, whose critique is all the stronger as he shares the anti-racist credentials and respect for diversity that underpin multiculturalism. In numerous articles and talks, Malik has brought an historical acuteness and anti-racist commitment to his attack on the various policies of multiculturalism. He analyses how multiculturalism has become politically seductive for governments keen to—or be seen to—address the inevitable problems of integration and social cohesion, but argues that the 'multiculturalist prescription creates the very problems it is meant to solve'. In its obsession with difference rather than commonality, culture rather than politics and ethnicity over and above any other kind of identity, the multiculturalism Malik describes is the kissing cousin of Neumann and Lasch-Quinn's US orthodoxy.

In appearing to offer respect for oppressed or marginalized groups, multicultural policy has resulted in a deeply conservative notion of tradition and cultural heritage that 'seeks self-consciously to yoke people to their identity for their own good'. Such an ideology has no place for universal values, perceived as neo-colonial Eurocentrism, and in place of a common political language legislates for sensitivity and a version of social solidarity based on separate ethnically bounded groups whose desires are voiced by self-styled 'community' representatives. Malik is scathing about the multicultural claims made by proponents such as Tariq Modood and Biku Parekh that 'respect' for other groups should be enforced, legally if necessary, as a minimum requirement for different groups to get along. On the contrary, he argues, this is to infantilize and patronize the members of subordinate groups. Offering them special treatment—not to speak of which form of belief or practice is to be respected and how this would be adjudicated—denies them the position of equal citizen and artificially protects them from the inevitable consequence of living in a free society: the possibility of being offended. As the Italian comedian Sabina Guzzanti, who was threatened with prosecution under arcane legalization for insulting the Pope, argues, excessive sensitivity to another's ideas amounts to 'treating him like an idiot who can't bear to hear an opinion different from his own. That is not necessarily respect' (see Hooper 2008).

Malik's *From Fatwa to Jihad* places such issues at the centre and is motivated by a powerful and very personal question: How did the young Asian activists, who were his friends and colleagues in the political struggles of the 1970s, become 'book burners' after the Rushdie fatwa and, in some cases, Islamist activists and the handmaids of terrorism? The answer lies in the way that UK multiculturalism, in the form of state sponsorship of groups or individuals claiming to speak for distinct cultural communities, enabled the rise of groups purporting to speak for British Muslims. In this capacity, they peddled a version of Islamic—in fact, the more extreme Islamist—identity that was compatible with the politics of identity and the compensatory and therapeutic practices they espoused. Islamic/Muslim extremism, empowered and financially supported by the UK government, offered disaffected radicals a powerful new form of political identity laced with the moral righteousness of victimhood and the promise of both psychic and material compensation. Neumann and many others have argued that modern Islamism and modern politically correct culture share an origin in the disappointments and fragmentations of the organized radical Left. Malik demonstrates the case by illuminating the path from left-wing activist to Islamist organizer. Whereas

the Socialist Workers' Party was doomed to
perennial marginality, over-hasty multiculturalism, scrambling to respond to the
threat of extremism, actually empowered
radical Islam by offering covert and not-so-
covert Islamists a place at high table. State-
sponsored Islamism—the state in question
being neither Saudi nor Iran but the UK—
offered a compelling new way of doing politics with government support. It brought
radicals in from the cold and offered them
genuine political power as long as their demands were packaged in the trappings of a
unique Muslim identity.

Malik details the way in which New
Labour, basing its actions on the belief that
'Muslims constitute a distinct community
with a distinct set of values and beliefs and
the real political authority for Muslims
must come from within the Muslim community,' from 1997 onwards 'contracted out' its
political obligations to the Muslim commu-

nity in the UK to a growing cadre of 'community leaders'. This meant that groups such as the Muslim Council of Britain, led by Iqbal Sacranie, with no mandate to speak for Muslims and no accountability to the diverse multinational entity that makes up the Muslim community in the UK, found themselves with hugely increased power and profile. Sacranie, Malik recalls, famously said of Rushdie that death would be 'a bit too easy for him'.

While I have been arguing that religion per se is not at the heart of contemporary claims of offence, and neither are they the exclusive preserve of Muslims, Islam is particularly fertile ground for the kind of victimhood that this modern piety articulates and encourages. For within Islam is a strong narrative of victimization, fuelled by a long history of frustration and defeat by the West. All the reiterations of the inevitability of Muslim triumph in the speeches of countless imams merely measure the distance between Muslim aspiration and Muslim achievement. There is no Islamic triumph, neither in the Arab world nor in the West. Islamism that claims it will bring one about draws support from those who would like to overcome their own sense of humiliation over this bald fact.

As *Newsnight* journalist Richard Watson's investigations into jihadi networks in the UK show—Watson summarized them in a long essay for *Granta* (2008)—figures like Omar Bakri Mohamed and Abu Hamza, who incredibly were invited into schools and colleges to address students in a misguided attempt to foster social harmony, were adept at recruiting disaffected, disappointed young men who were not necessarily religious zealots but were fuelled by a sense of resentment towards a West that had frustrated their attempts to succeed on its terms—as international cricketer, drug-dealer, lover or teacher—and whose very economic and political superiority to the Islamic world was an affront to their own fragile sense of identity. Bakri Mohamed and his ilk worked on these boys, showing them videos of the slaughter of Muslims in Bosnia and Chechnya, always grooming and looking for the outstanding recruit or perfect patsy, stoking up their outrage and sense of personal and group hurt. 'Humiliation,' as the philosopher Tzvetan Todorov has written, 'is a powerful motive for violent acts' (2007).

It needs to be emphasized that this is a very modern version of religion. Members of the radical Islamist group Hizb-ut Tahrir, for example, explicitly saw themselves as turning against the traditional, quiescent and moderate religion of their parents. They rejected arranged marriages, believing one should marry for love, and turned to the resources of the Quran filtered

through modern interpretations such as
that of Said Qutb, the ideologue of the
Muslim Brotherhood, who also drew on the
political ideas of the Marxist Antonio
Gramsci and of Nazism. This form of
radical Islam is a markedly modern political
religious movement, with more emphasis
on politics than theology. As the jihad
scholar Hegghammer argues, those turning
to the speeches of Osama Bin Laden ex-
pecting to hear religious ranting will be disappointed: 'there are no complex
theological arguments'. Instead:

> Bin Laden's discourse is profoundly
> political and elegant in its simplicity.
> It is populism at its most effective and
> most frightening.

His central theme 'is the suffering and humiliation of the Muslim nation at the hands
of non-Muslims'.

The problem, of course, is when this
humiliation, resentment and violent rage

comes into contact with the kind of offensive material that is part and parcel of free speech in the West. Satire, mockery, parody and filth are an essential part of the arsenal of cultural criticism and debate in the West, part of what marks it out from autocracies and totalitarian states, especially those of the Muslim world. The freedom to offend and blaspheme has been hard won and is rightly cherished. But inevitably, when the satirical pen or brush is turned on a target like Islam, it triggers the kind of violent reaction in the men of resentment that led to the murder of Theo Van Gogh, the violent protests against the Danish cartoons, the murder of Rushdie's translator and the pathetically ineffective attempt by three Muslim men in September 2008 to burn down the house of the publisher of *The Jewel of Medina*. The question, then, is how we, the Western media, should respond.

One answer is: not with more piety.

A significant trend that emerged in response to the Danish cartoons crisis was the strong statement of the fundamental and absolute right to freedom of expression. Among the proponents of such a view were some of our most erudite and influential cultural commentators, including novelists Salman Rushdie and Martin Amis, ubiquitous journalist Christopher Hitchens, *The Times* columnist Oliver Kamm and *Observer* columnist and author Nick Cohen. These writers and many others rallied to the call to defend freedom of speech against censorship either by the state or through the threat of violence and intimidation (see, especially, Kamm 2007). And very stirring these defences were, like these ringing words from Hitchens in 'Cartoon Debate: The Case for Mocking Religion' published by *Slate* in February 2006:

> Can discussion be carried on without the threat of violence, or the automatic response to it? . . .Civil society

means that free expression trumps
the emotions of anyone to whom free
expression might be inconvenient.

Such, too, was the position of Flemming Rose the *Jyllands-Posten* editor who commissioned the cartoons. But his justification for doing so was not, or not entirely, about celebrating the right to offend. It was, he said, an attempt to 'open up a debate about Islam and the West' and to fight the insidious rise of self-censorship in the light of a cancellation of a screening of Theo Van Gogh's film *Submission* (2004) at the European Parliament.

Thus one form of piety is met with another: that of the fearless Western press ever-willing to stand firm against threats to their right to say what they like. As Jeremy Harding wrote in the *London Review of Books*, also in February 2006:

> [T]here is something tacky and melo-
> dramatic about European editors
> rediscovering self-censorship as a sin-

ister, internalised instruction that
holds them back from the fullness of
democratic genius.

This, Harding avers, is to miss the fact
that 'self-censorship' in the guise of judgement could equally be thought of as acu-
men, and it allows the Western media to
worship 'at the shrine of their own self-
importance'. The strutting of Wilders, Rose
and the controversialist Mark Steyn, those
calculating crusaders in the battle to save
Christendom, whose attempts to enrage
Muslim sentiment bear all the marks of a
self-fulfilling prophecy, is surely offensive to
more than just the thin-skinned Muslim.

Such figures love to project themselves
as the lonely outposts of reason and
courage, endlessly patting themselves and
others on the back for having the balls to
risk the wrath of Islam and stand against
the timid relativist appeasers who dominate
the media. Yet this heroic few is quite a sub-

stantial portion of the Anglo-US media, including high profile columnists and writers—Melanie Phillips, Nick Cohen, Theodore Dalrymple—backed by conservative publications such as *The City Journal*, *Standpoint*, *The New York Sun* and *The New Criterion*, reinforced by virulent right-wing bloggers such as Daniel Pipes, Stanley Kurtz, Bruce Bawer and Robert Spencer, and funded and supported by thinktanks and foundations such as The Hudson Institute and The Social Affairs Unit. Neoconservatism may have lost its immediate influence on US foreign policy but its influence has never been stronger on the debate about Islam and the West, and it is as effective an exploiter of the Internet as radical Islam. It is a digitally enabled, 24-hour and largely free access to clash of pieties.

And in among all the assertions of the absolute right to freedom of speech there is very little recognition of the daily operation of media self-censorship, where a myriad of forces, from economic and political considerations to social or legal niceties and the influence of PR and spin, to the operations of taste and editorial judgement, may limit what a journalist is allowed or willing to say. On a wide range of subjects from anti-Semitism to paedophilia the media quite rightly operates within self-imposed limits, based not on the pre-existing right not to be offended by any one group, but on the judgement about what are legitimate targets for scrutiny, satire or mockery. For the practising media, the question is not 'what am I allowed to say', but 'what should be said and with what aim'. If we judge the actions of *Jyllands-Posten* by this standard, for example, we have to assess whether the cartoons were the best way to stimulate a debate about the relationship between Islam and the West, rather than, as Todorov has argued, a form of 'entrapment' which produced an entirely predictable response and made no contribution at all to free and open debate.

The implication that, before the hyper-sensitive Muslims popped up, the Western media was a Shangri-La of freedom and publish-and-be-damned muck-raking is simply false and looks like a conscious attempt to manufacture the case for the fundamental incompatibility of Islam and Western liberal values. And if it is true to say that the relativist multiculturalism of the 'Guardianista' has been the intellectual orthodoxy of the past decades, then there has been a substantial shift since then to arguments about why we must be uncompromising in our response to Islam, violence and threats to freedom of speech.

This line of argument also tends to literalism, the assumption that if someone does something in the name of Islam, then that is why they did it; that if one Muslim claims to speak for all then that is what they

are doing. Thus do extremisms reinforce
each other. It bears repetition that not all
Muslims were offended by the Muhammad
cartoons, and that those who were and
expressed their outrage in public, even
holding 'offensive' banners criticizing the
West, were exercising their right as citizens
of the free West. It is when this tips over
into violence or the threat of violence that a
line is crossed, but turning the volume up
on pieties about the absolute right to free
speech is likely to have as much effect on
preventing Islamic violence as blasting a
sample of 'All You Need is Love' from loud-
speakers on the streets of Brixton would
have on preventing knife crime.

So much for the pieties of absolute free
expression.

But an even more dangerous form of
piety has sprouted in the wake of 9/11 and
the Muhammad cartoons. It is symbolized
in the UK by the magazine *Standpoint*,

launched in 2008 by the right-wing think-tank, Social Affairs Unit, and edited by the journalist Daniel Johnson. *Standpoint*, Johnson declares in the inaugural issue, has a simple purpose—the defence of Western civilization. And what is this Western civilization apart from, as Gandhi noted, 'a very good idea'? For Johnson, it is embattled, in need of defence and celebration, 'overwhelmingly benign' and a confluence of the Classical and the Judaeo-Christian. The reason why Western civilization is in need of this new, firm standpoint is because 'we have seen not only our technology but our laws and liberties . . . exploited by the enemies of the open society'. It won't surprise you to learn that chief among these enemies are the Islamists—the cover story for *Standpoint*'s first issue was historian Michael Burleigh's call for the war on terror to be prosecuted with more vigour—but not only them. As Johnson made explicit at a conference on 'Soft *jihad*', sponsored by *Standpoint* and the Hudson Institute in London (September 2008), the list also includes the enemies within, the 'militant atheists' who are 'doing the work of the Islamists' by 'undermining Christendom'.

This follows the line currently being pedalled by the Hudson Institute and argued, for example, by Paul Belien, who wrote in the *Washington Times* in 2008: 'The secularists have created a religious vacuum in the heart of European society—which Islam is filling.' The consequences of reading contemporary history as having reached final showdown between Western values—interpreted as secular and liberal when it suits them, or as Judaeo-Christian when that is expedient—is that it licences the kind of nonsense that Douglas Murray, author of the book *Neoconservatism*: *Why We Need It* (2007) and Director of the Centre for Social Cohesion, feels able to argue as

he did in a piece for the *Spectator* in 2007
We should be unafraid to announce that
'our' way was 'the only way to live' and 'our'
values 'superior to all others', he wrote. It
would be impolite, or perhaps hopelessly
relativist, to note such trifles as colonialism
or imperialism, catastrophic inequality or
the exporting of capitalism at the barrel of
a gun. But it is worth reminding the cele-
brators of the Judaeo-Christian West that
'Western culture' is, in the words of the
philosopher Christophe Türcke, as much
built from, 'the conquering of large parts of
America, Africa and Asia', including plenty
of genocide and plundering of natural resources. It was gold and silver, cotton and
sugar, coffee, rubber and oil from these
countries that created the material means
for the West to become what it is. 'Without
this basis,' Türcke argues, 'human rights
such as freedom of expression, of the press,
of religion . . . would never have got a
chance' (2006).

Talk of *our* culture, *their* intolerance, *our* liberties, *their* violence, when attached to Judaeo-Christian celebration of the West does not account for how much Islam, another conquering creed that mirrors Christianity, shares with the West, including the bellicose language of culture clash. If such ahistorical triumphalism is all we can offer in the face of threats to free speech, can we be surprised that a sense of humiliation and hurt pride is on the rise among young Muslims? We need to hold even tighter to our values when they are under threat but not by projecting an image of the West as both dominant and deservedly so, superior and possessed of a superiority complex to boot, and everything that a Muslim isn't and cannot hope to be—not just modern, free and tolerant, but Judaeo-Christian as well. This strikes me both as impractical and immoral.

A tendency that goes hand in hand with the projection of Europe as Judaeo-Chris-

tian and, therefore, in the words of one
prominent Dutch blogger 'no place for
Muslims', is scaremongering about Europe's
'ticking demographic timebomb'. Soon, we
are warned, the higher birth rate of Muslim
immigrants will give them unprecedented
power to turn 'our' democracy against 'us'
and the battle will be lost. But such an argument, made by the likes of Mark Styen and
Geert Wilders, much enamoured of Europe's Christian roots, betrays an extraordinary lack of confidence in a system whose
superiority they trumpet so loudly and a
particular disregard for democracy. To
imagine that all Muslims living in Europe,
and the unborn millions to come, will necessarily be immune to the appeal of freedom and tolerance and mutual respect with
which we are all educated suggests a lack of
belief in the persuasiveness of these values,
or a lack of attention to the millions of European Muslims who live by these values
every day. The idea that all Muslims will

vote with their religion and hasten the end
of society as we know it, betrays an idea of
culture and identity as conservative, fixed
and ahistorical as that which underpins
al-Qaeda's desire to 'restore' a Caliphate
that existed for a total of 15 years more
than 1,200 years ago. And to deny in ad-
vance any group, on the basis of one aspect
of their identity, the right to exercise their
political rights when their time comes by
suggesting that you know how they will vote
and you don't like it, is as authoritarian as
any threat to the West from without.

A MEDIA MANIFESTO

Since this book is presented as part of a series of manifestos, I'd like to finish with a
modest practical proposal for how the
media should negotiate these choppy wa-
ters. As I have said, I am a secular journalist
and editor with a huge debt to and stake in

freedom of expression. Nothing would be more disastrous for me professionally and personally than to be limited to publishing material that would never offend anyone. Some accuse critics of absolutist arguments as being 'liberals who proclaim it morally unacceptable to give offence'. The words are those of Kenan Malik writing in *The Times* on the *Jewel of Medina* case in September 2008. This does not apply to me. I agree with John Stuart Mill that giving offence is essential if   society is to challenge its orthodoxies and put power under proper scrutiny. It's also a lot of fun. But, although we should never be prevented from publishing anything because it might be offensive, or suffer violence or the threat of violence, we still have to exercise judgement about what we publish and when. And an aspect of this will be the awareness of who we are offending and why.

To this end I offer a five-point plan:

(1) Offend the powerful, defend the weak. Offensiveness is a potent weapon to be used wisely. Shun fashionable targets.

There is nothing surprising or brave about riling up the humiliated. Taking offence, as J. M. Coetzee argues in his book *Giving Offense: Essays on Censorship* (1996), is pre-eminently a tool used by the powerless, one of the only avenues they have for being heard. Those with other sources of self-confidence can easily overlook it; it is those with little else but their fragile sense of identity who resent and retaliate against in-sult. Of course, there are those—like the chorus of spurious human rights organiza-tions claiming to speak for minority feel-ings—who will fan and incite the emotions of the powerless wherever possible. The latter are a legitimate target for satire, the former, in my view, are not. Complicated isn't it? The exercise of free expression in this messy context requires not the relin-

quishing of discrimination, or the retrench-
ment of fundamental principles, but better
judgement.

(2) Don't get conned into supporting self-
styled champions of freedom who consciously provoke outrage in order to boast
of their martyrdom. If we are forced to defend their right not to be slain for whatever
idiotic thing they do, we equally need to be
rigorous in our condemnation of acts of
calculated offensiveness.

In 2005, I was put under some pressure
to put the Danish cartoons on the front
cover of *New Humanist*, to express solidarity
with *Jyllands-Posten* and an absolute commitment to free speech. I resisted these calls
for a whole range of reasons that could look
like self-censorship or cowardice but were,
I felt, the everyday judgements of publishing. I didn't like the cartoons aesthetically;
I didn't generate the cartoons myself so
they were not part of my editorial strategy;

I wasn't party to the process of their creation or to the context in which they were produced; I was unconvinced that the undoubted controversy that would be generated by my doing so would be justified or a good thing for the magazine; most of all, I didn't want anyone else's agenda to hijack my editorial autonomy. Many free-speech zealots castigated small magazine editors like myself for refusing to republish the cartoons and *Granta*'s then editor Ian Jack for writing about why he didn't. They said we were cowardly. My response is that I reserve the right to offend who I want when I want, but that doesn't mean I have to endorse every act of calculated offensiveness. If Flemming Rose, who commissioned the cartoons, was sincere in wanting to start a debate about self-censorship in the media— rather than triggering a wave of outrage and recrudescence of absolutisms—then they were an undoubted failure.

(3) Do your own offending. Don't piggy back on the offensiveness of others, and start with your own audience

The most controversial cover of *New Humanist* during my tenure as editor was the one featuring arch-atheist Richard Dawkins (see frontispiece to this book). We received some complaints directly and many others were posted on Richard Dawkins' own website. Some atheists felt we had insulted Dawkins by trivializing his campaign for atheists to 'out' themselves; others because we had, they claimed, depicted him as a gay stereotype; and even others because they felt we had insulted them personally by presenting Dawkins' supporters as mindless sheep. All-in-all a most satisfying result. It raised the profile of the magazine and the article to which it referred—Richard Norman's critique of the New Atheists—and allowed for a lively debate, much of it online, within which all the various perspectives of non-belief had their say, including those who pointed out that it was somewhat ironic that so many 'free thinking' people had become offended because of perceived criticism of the patron saint of atheism. We need more of the kind of satiric offensiveness that is addressed to the core audience, the home team, your own kind, rather than aimed at the out-sider, the—implicitly over-testy—foreigner, anyone but ourselves.

(4) Concentrate on what really matters—unfair legislation for instance—and build coalitions to challenge the tools the power-ful use to avoid scrutiny and punish free expression.

Rather than follow in the wake of the extremist baiters hollering about the ab-solute right to offend, there are pressing issues around which a broad coalition of free-speech supporters can mobilize. Free-speechers from all sides of the political spectrum, from Robert Spencer at *Jihad-Watch* to Jo Glanville at *Index on Censorship*, can, for example, push forward on legal reform.

Our civic and legal frameworks have made themselves vulnerable to abuse by those claiming offence because we have allowed it. The recent emergence of a new threat to free speech in the form of 'Soft *jihad*'—the use by Islamic radicals of Western law to prevent criticism or investigation of their activities—is genuine and we need to guard against it by strengthening the fundamental, though necessarily minimal, values of an open society. In one well-known case, Cambridge University Press was forced by the UK courts to withdraw, pulp and apologize for references to the Saudi Banker Khalid bin Mahfouz in the book *Alms for Jihad: Charity and Terrorism in the Islamic World* (2006) by the US authors Robert O. Collins and J. Millard Burr. The book suggested Mahfouz was behind a number of charities that had helped to fund terrorism. Mahfouz, a very rich man, threatened legal action under UK libel law, where the burden of proof is on the accused. Rather than be dragged into the potentially expensive action, Cambridge University Press withdrew the book and paid substantial damages. According to Rachel Ehrenfeld, a journalist who has been sued by Mahfouz on a number of occasions, Mahfouz has successfully blocked the publication of 41 books in this way.

Here is precisely the kind of concrete threat to free expression, uncontaminated by the taint of entrapment or the issue of personal sensitivity, around which those who support free speech can rally. The threat in this area comes every bit as much from other powerful interest groups—such as the Church of Scientology, which has been successful in silencing dissent through the threat of legal repercussions—as it does from jihadis. Libel law in the UK has always been stacked in favour of the rich and powerful, and it is time it was reviewed or abolished. Critically, the issue here is defence of the right to speak the truth, not the rather more subjective and easily abused right to insult.

We also need to look at the restrictions on free expression that are in place, right now, across Europe. The UK Racial and Religious Hatred Act of 2006, though much diluted, still affords undue protection to religious belief and does little to protect the truly vulnerable; Article 166 of the German legal code forbids 'causing insult to faiths, religious communities and groups of people sharing the same view of the world'; as mentioned earlier, the law against showing 'contempt for the Pope' was invoked to threaten Sabina Guzzanti with prosecution. International structures are not immune from this kind of manipulation either. The

UN Resolution on 'Combating Defamation of Religion' is sponsored by the 57-nation Organisation of Islamic Conference (OIC) and has been ratified each year since 2005. Many, like the European Centre for Law and Justice, now fear that the resolution is being used as a way to head-off legitimate criticism of the human rights record of some of the member states and to justify religious discrimination, such as the punitive blasphemy laws in Egypt, Pakistan and Sudan.

(5) Can we all just grow up?

If we pour scorn on benighted and intolerant Islam unable to take a joke and eager to exclude aspects of its sacred identity from mockery or even open debate, we must similarly be alive to our own promotion of identity as destiny, our fetishization of individual rights, and inflation of the idea that we should be protected from insult. The pious of all stripes trade on the idea that we are 'embedded' within a certain culture and identity and with a fixed relation to the sacred. Our society must take its secularism more seriously than this: we must value the right to think for ourselves, to transcend the entrapments of 'identity' and the glorifications of suffering. We need to get over the idea that we all deserve respect, protection from insult or, indeed, happiness. We must take responsibility for our own feelings, not ask for the government or the law to protect them, and both respect and happiness must be earned. We can't all have them, but we can all try.

The 'free' West has to get its house in order before delivering lectures on the tolerance of free expression to anyone else. Governments must shoulder part of the burden too—and not by promoting rigid or romantic forms of national identity to match those already in play, but by emphasizing the openness of citizenship and the rights and responsibilities that come with it.

They must get out of the business of legis-
lating against perceived psychic harm and
of promoting intermediaries through whom
to communicate to their own citizens.

We all need the courage to believe that
the basic values of our civilization will hold
because they work best and are why people
come here in the first place. In the end, we
can do very little about those who want to
use violence and intimidation, be it
drunken murderers on the streets of Nor-
wich or jihadis firebombing publishers. We
must support the police and security serv-
ices in working against these people on behalf of us all. Meanwhile, our concern is
and must be with everyone else: how to
make our version of the nation wide
enough to include both different ethnic and
religious groups and those already here,
marginalized and forgotten.

Those who, like me, support free
speech are fond of quoting George Orwell's

line from the preface to *Animal Farm* (1945)—a book he had great trouble getting published—about the fact that true liberty means being able to tell people what they don't want to hear. These are vital words, but we would do well to remember another passage from the same essay that reminds us that 'Tolerance and decency are deeply rooted in England, but they are not indestructible, and they have to be kept alive partly by conscious effort.'

One of Martin Rowson's many 'offensive' cartoons for *New Humanist*.

BIBLIOGRAPHY

AMIS, Martin. 2008. *The Second Plane*: *September 11, 2001–2007*. London: Jonathan Cape.

BELIEN, Paul. 2008. 'Islamofascism in the Netherlands'. *Washington Times* (21 May).

COETZEE, J. M. 1996. *Giving Offense*: *Essays on Censorship*. Chicago: University of Chicago Press.

COLLINS, Robert O. and J. Millard Burr. 2006. *Alms for Jihad*: *Charity and Terrorism in the Islamic World*. New York, NY: Cambridge University Press.

ENZENSBURGER, Hans Magnus. 2005. 'The Radical Loser'. *signandsight.com* (1 December; first published in German in *Der Speigel*, 7 November).

GLANVILLE, Jo. 2008. 'Respect for Religion Now Makes Censorship the Norm'. *Guardian* (30 September).

HARDING, Jeremy. 2006. 'Short Cuts'. *London Review of Books* (23 February).

HEGGHAMMER, Thomas. 2008. 'Jihadi Studies'. *Times Literary Supplement* (2 April).

———. *Jihad in Saudi Arabia*: *Violence and Pan-Islamism since 1979*. 2009. New York, NY: Cambridge University Press, forthcoming (Autumn).

HIGGINS, Andrew. 2008. 'Why Islam is Unfunny for One Cartoonist'. *Wall Street Journal* (12 July).

HITCHENS, Christopher. 2006. 'Cartoon Debate: The Case for Mocking Religion'. *Slate* (4 February).

HOEKSTRA, Peter. 2007. 'Islam and Free Speech'. *Wall Street Journal* (26 March).

HOOPER, John. 2008. 'Dangerously Funny: Interview with Sabina Guzzanti'. *Guardian* (29 September).

HULL, Gloria T., Patricia Bell Scott and Barbara Smith (eds). 1982. *All the Blacks are Men. All the Women are White. But Some of Us are Brave*. New York, NY: Feminist Press at The City University of New York.

JAMES, George G. 1993. *Stolen Legacy*: *Greek Philosophy is Stolen Egyptian Philosophy*. Trenton, NJ: Africa World Press.

JOHNSON, Daniel. 2008. 'Editorial'. *Standpoint* (June).

KAMM, Oliver. 2007. 'The Tyranny of Moderation: Respect and Civility are the Enemies of Free Speech'. *The Times* (22 May).

KIRSCH, Adam. 2008. 'The Writing Man's Burden' *New York Sun* (26 March).

LARSEN, Nella. 1929. *Passing*. New York: Modern Library.

LASCH-QUINN, Elisabeth. 2001. *Race Experts: How Racial Etiquette, Sensitivity Training, and New Age Therapy Hijacked the Civil Rights Revolution.* New York: W. W. Norton and Company.

——. 2006. 'Identity Crisis'. *New Humanist* (January/February).

LEBOR, Adam. 2008. 'The UN Human Rights Council: Not Fit for Purpose'. *Standpoint* (15 September).

LEFKOWITZ, Mary. 2008. *History Lesson: A Race Odyssey*. New Haven, CT: Yale University Press.

MALIK, Kenan. 2005. 'Making A Difference: Culture, Race and Social Policy'. *Patterns of Prejudice* 39(4) (December).

———. 2006. 'Clashes and Conflicts from *At the Turning of the Tide*'. Centre For Racial Equality.

———. 2007. 'The Importance of Giving Offence'. *Index on Censorship* (8 January).

———. 2008. 'Self-censor and Be Damned!' *The Times* (29 September).

———. 2009. *From Fatwa to Jihad: The Rushdie Affair and Its Legacy*. USA: Atlantic Books, forthcoming (Spring).

MAYES, Tessa. 2008. 'Mill is a Dead White Male with Something to Say.' *Spiked-online.com* (28 March).

MILLER, Laura. 2008. 'Terror and Loathing'. A review of *The Second Plane*. *Salon.com* (2 April).

MONGIN, Olivier, Nathalie Lempereur and Jean-Louis Schlegel. 2006. 'What is Postcolonial Thinking? An Interview with Achille Mbembe'. *Spirit* (December).

MURRAY, Douglas. 2007. 'Don't Be Afraid to Say It'. *Spectator* (3 October).

———. 2007. *Neoconservatism: Why We Need It*. UK: Encounter Books.

———. 2008. 'A Film-maker Who Lives in the Shadow of Fatwa'. Spectator.co.uk (2 April).

NEUMANN, Michael. 2006. 'Respectful Cultures and Disrespectful Cartoons, East Meets West'. *Counterpunch.org* (13 February).

ORWELL, George. 1945. *Animal Farm*. London: Secker and Warburg.

OWEN, Ursula. 2006. 'Getting Used to Offence'. A speech to the conference on Media and Good Governance, Amman, 14–16 February. *Eurozine.com*

RAUCH, Jonathan. 1993. *Kindly Inquisitors*. Chicago: University of Chicago Press.

RUSHDIE, Salman. 1991. 'In Good Faith', in *Imaginary Homelands: Essays and Criticism 1981–1991*. London: Granta Books.

SCOTT, Joan. 2008. Forced To Be Free'. *New Humanist* (March/April).

STAFF WRITERS. 2008. 'Civil Rights Activists Criticise UN Religious Defamation Resolution'. *Ekklesia.co.uk* (2 September).

TAYLOR, Charles. 1992. 'The Politics of Recognition', in *Multiculturalism and the*

Politics of Recognition. Princeton: Princeton University Press.

TODOROV, Tzvetan. 2007. 'Global Warning'. *New Humanist* (November/December).

TÜRCKE, Christoph. 2006. 'Blasphemy: On the Structure of Mass Insult', *Eurozine* (first published in German, *Merkur* 6).

WATSON, Richard. 2008. 'The One True God Allah'. *Granta* 103 (Autumn).

VARIOUS. 2008. *Free Speech in the Age of Jihad*. Special pamphlet published by *New Criterion* (July).